Wendy Harmer wrote this and feels a lot better now, thanks.

Bruce Currie is an animator/illustrator whom the author encountered when he was face-down in a seedy bar surrounded by empty scotch bottles. She immediately recognised him as a kindred spirit.

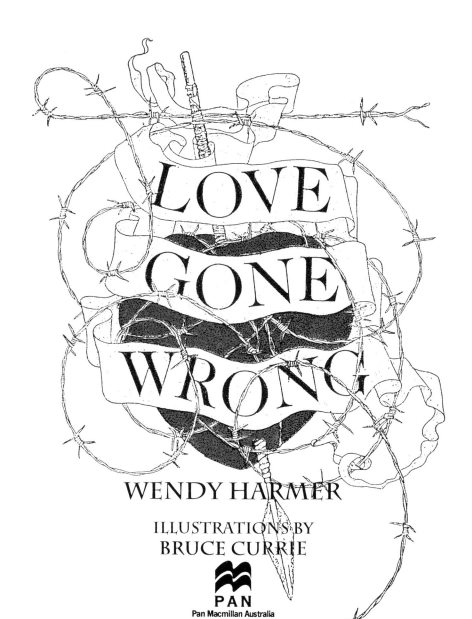

LOVE GONE WRONG

WENDY HARMER

ILLUSTRATIONS BY
BRUCE CURRIE

PAN
Pan Macmillan Australia

For the X's

First published 1991 in Macmillan by Pan Macmillan Australia Pty Limited

This Pan edition first published 1995 by Pan Macmillan Australia Pty Limited
St Martins Tower, 31 Market Street, Sydney

National Library of Australia
cataloguing-in-publication data:

Harmer, Wendy,
Love gone wrong.

ISBN 0 330 35773 5.

1. Love – Humor. 2. Love – Anecdotes.
3. Australian wit and humor.
I. Currie, Bruce. II. Title.

A828.302

Typeset in Bembo by Midland Typesetters
Printed in Australia by Griffin Colour

These words will give no solace to you, the brokenhearted, but remember, you are not alone. In every major city in the country, on any given evening, there are at least 100,000 people under the influence of cheap alcohol driving like maniacs to their Ex-lover's place to demand: 'WHAT THE BLOODY HELL'S GOING ON?'

You see at school we learned about homemaking. The boys made a matchstick tray in their Woodwork class; the girls set a tray for afternoon tea in Domestic Science. But we were never taught how to cope if the happy home came apart. That's what Domestic Science should have been about . . . domestics.

When hearts break they hurt. The cry of those who are feeling the pain of shattered love is: 'This hurts so much. Why didn't someone tell me about this?' Well, dear reader, consider yourself told.

Here they are . . . Fragments of a Broken Heart. If you can reassemble them you'll find a way through.

I once met a person who had never had a broken heart. He looked like a fat, happy grub sitting in a rotten apple. When I tried to explain, he said: 'Don't worry, you'll get over it, time heals all, there're plenty more fish in the sea, there's no use crying over spilt milk, you should be glad it happened now, it'll all be for the best in the long run.' I knew that even in the long run time would not heal crying over spilt fish. Watching him wriggle away, I had the feeling that in the end he might just turn into a fat, happy moth.

Centuries ago 'griefe' was a notifiable disease. In 1657 Dr Heberden catalogued the causes of death in London as:

Flox and Small Pox	835
Found dead in the streets etc.	9
French Pox	25
Griefe	10
Griping and Plague in the Guts	446
Hang'd and made away 'emselves	24

Ladies took to their beds, with draughts of laudanum, where they sickened and withered away. Men joined the Foreign Legion and threw themselves at the enemy with no regard for personal safety. Maiden aunts took their heartbroken charges on trips to Europe and India by slow steamer. But in this disposable age friends will tell you your heart can be mended with a frivolous hat, a good party and a new love.

When your heart is broken the world breaks up too. The planet you both lived on has been nuked and is now littered with the fragments of favourite songs and the ruins of special restaurants. The landscapes you both admired are toxic wastelands. You feel like a shadow or one of those cartoon characters with a black cloud of gloom drawn over its head. If you walk past a happy couple they feel a melancholy spell cast on them and they snuggle closer together for protection.

'If you love somebody set them free' says the pop song. A sentiment better suited to Californian therapists. Let's get Clint Eastwood back into the picture, you say. Go round to your Ex's place with a 44 Magnum. 'You . . . and the bitch . . . on the floor . . . bang, bang.' Let's face it you'll feel better, he won't know what hit him and who gives a damn what she thinks. Yes!

'No, forgive and forget,' say your friends. So you think you'll ring the new couple and tell them how happy you are for them. Four o'clock in the morning would be a good time—at ten minute intervals. For the next six months.

You'll put on weight, take it off, cry at advertisements for bathroom accessories, drink too much, let pot plants die, shout at relatives, leave the telephone off the hook, crash the car and forget to pay the rent.

But remember that people who have never had a broken heart will never understand dead roses, Tolstoy, airport lounges, Albinoni's 'Adagio in G Minor', neat brandy, the moon or drizzle.

You WILL get over it! One day you realise there really is a cosmic scheme to things when you are walking arm in arm with your gorgeous new lover and there is your Ex, lying in the gutter, surrounded by empty port bottles, mumbling: 'I was wrong, I was wrong, forgive me.'

WHEN THEY SAY	**THEY MEAN** ....
I want to be by myself.	Well, we can't both sleep with my new girlfriend, can we?
I need more space.	There's not enough room in the bed for three and she likes to move around a lot.
I need some time to think things over.	I'd rather be out of the house when I ring the removal van.
We're just not suited to each other.	She's ten years younger than you.
I didn't mean to hurt you.	I wanted to kill you.
We've just drifted apart.	I can't stand the sight of you.
This has nothing to do with you.	It's got everything to do with that Russian weightlifter I'm seeing.
I'm the one who's to blame.	I'm going to make you feel as guilty as possible.
All I want is for you to be happy.	I've told all my friends you have psychiatric problems.
You'll have no trouble finding someone else.	If you go near any of my girlfriends I'll smash your windscreen with an empty scotch bottle.
When you get over this I'd really like you to meet Brian, you'd get along really well.	When Brian takes me skiing in Switzerland, you can look after the cat.
I miss you.	I may kill myself.

I'm fine . . . really.	My life is in ruins and I hope you feel like a piece of shit.
Everyone's been great.	Your best friend put the hard word on me last night.
The family sends their love.	The family is sending over a hit man.

I'm not seeing anyone in particular.	I'm sleeping with everyone in general.
Let's give it another go.	I still have some self esteem left.
Maybe we could get together and have a drink.	Maybe we could get together and have a drink and fight like we used to—but let's do it in public this time in case you're not humiliated enough.
Maybe we could see a counsellor.	Let's spend our life savings on finding out why we're not compatible.
There'll never be anyone else like you.	I will never make the same horrific mistake again.
I'd still like to be friends.	I'd like to hang around long enough to ruin your next relationship.

Today I'm going to start living my life to the full. It's a single life . . . rich with possibility. I'm going to treat myself to a walk in the park. This is just for me. Look, the sun is out, how it warms me up. It's great to be alive. Those trees, they're magnificent. Trees are single, they don't need each other. You don't see trees arm in arm, leaning on one another, do you? No, trees are the perfect symbol of strength and independence.

I'll sit here and look at the grass, the flowers. I don't think I've ever seen them with such clarity before. I've been asleep, under a blanket of security. Life is an adventure again.

A jogger . . . where's he going? Down life's highway, a lone traveller. Like me. You can't really jog when you're with other people . . . it's like life . . . someone's always lagging behind or urging you to catch up. 'Hello . . . lovely day!'

Over there, that drunken derro. Just goes to show, there's always someone worse off than yourself. He probably knew the pain of a broken heart once and gave in to it. Not me. I'm back on top of life, alone and feeling great. Treelike.

Look at that bird. It's alone, free . . . oh there're two of them. They're nesting. I wonder if they mate for life? But then again birds are driven by pure instinct, they need mates. They haven't the capacity for independent thought like . . . trees.

Ha ha, there's a fat old lady rolling around on the grass. She's free, she's happy just being in her own company. Look at her big fat legs, three legs, she's got three, she's got four legs. It's a couple. They're rolling around on the grass . . . look at them laughing. They're laughing because they love each other. It's really pathetic the way they're carrying on right in front of everybody. In front of that couple on the bench—kissing. Oh God, they're kissing. Look, there're two more over there holding hands.

I'm the only one in this park who's alone.

I'm staying here, I've got a right to be here by myself under my tree. Look at this pigeon. I'll feed this pigeon here. Lonely, are you, boy? Yeah, you and me and the tree. We understand, don't we? You want some crumbs, eh? A few crumbs, we're entitled to that at least, aren't we? A few crumbs of affection. Yeah, share it with your little friend. Hey, hey! Stop that! Get off her! Filthy little beasts!

Am I the only one in this whole stupid park who isn't in love or lust or . . . oh shut up! What would you know, you're only a stupid lump of wood.

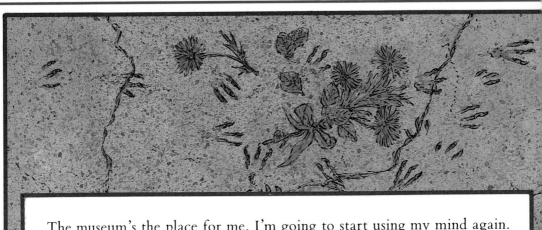

The museum's the place for me. I'm going to start using my mind again. I'll devote myself to the world of knowledge, become a scholar. There are higher callings in life than being in some brain-dead relationship.

Maybe I'll become a geologist. Look at these rocks. Rocks are wonderful, they have absolutely no feelings at all. It must feel good to be a rock. It would be great to be out in the desert, far away from anyone, digging up ancient civilizations. I could be an archaeologist. The only people I'd see would have been dead for thousands of years. I'd dig up artefacts like these old pots here. Look at the amazing detail on these ancient pots, people dancing, writhing together . . . copulating.

What are these funny old statues over here? Look, this one's carrying a spear. No, it isn't . . . it's a phallus. My God, I haven't seen anything like that since . . . ah, here she is. A big fat happy woman. She's pregnant. I don't believe this—I'm surrounded by fertility symbols.

Dinosaurs, that's what I'd like to dig up. A Tyrannosaurus Rex with huge flesh-tearing teeth, crushing everything in its path. I could dig up a mammoth, except that I'd have to dig up two mammoths because, here they are, Mr and Mrs Mammoth. Christ, look at this, even a big ugly hairy mammoth can get a mate. Get me out of here!

Oh look at this, it's so beautiful: a single cell amoeba. It's single . . . it's single!

There's no better place to do something for yourself than at the gym. It's pure self-indulgence. I don't have to look at anybody else. My mind is focused on these machines, pulling, pushing. I'm just one big muscle. There's no brain. A strong body . . . that's what I'm after.

If I were looking for a new lover a taut physique would be an advantage. But I'm doing this for myself, this is for me, for my eyes only. Who knows, I might make myself so beautiful that when I get home I'll take advantage of myself—stick my tongue down my own throat. I don't think that's exactly what my therapist had in mind when she talked about 'self-love', but it's not a bad idea. Look at me in that mirror. I look great. How could anyone not love me? Don't answer that question. Just keep pulling, pushing. Pushing, pulling . . . it's amazing how even a little exercise can make you so aware of your body . . . the perspiration on my neck, running down my back, behind my knees . . . this feels almost as good as an afternoon of . . . pushing, pulling.

What I need now is a massage to help me wind down. It'll be good for me. From now on I'm going to indulge my every whim. Yes, that feels great, those hands stroking me, soothing me. It's a long time since I felt anyone's hands on me. In fact the last time was . . . forget it.

I have to pay someone to touch me! They don't care, they're probably thinking about their lover at this very moment. I wonder if they find my body repulsive. I hate this. Take your filthy hands off me, you'll just use me and in forty-five minutes, I'll be just a memory. Oh God, I feel so cheap!

No matter what happens it's important to keep the basic functions of life going. I have to sleep. I have to eat. I have to go to the laundromat. You can't let yourself go. You've got to have clean clothes. Now then, just the one machine, just the one towel, just the one . . . pillowcase. It's so easy doing the washing these days. No arguments about which cycle, bleach or no bleach. No-one's colours will run into my whites. Just my socks, my hankies and my underwear, uncontaminated by anyone else's waste. I feel quite self contained, like my little washing tub here.

Ha, look at that machine there. They've thrown all their stuff in together. It'll probably all come out grey. Look at those bra straps strangling those jocks. Take a week to get them untangled. Take that couple forever to get their lives untangled . . . their grey lives.

That's a suspender belt writhing around with that string vest . . . and they look like crotchless knickers . . . tumbling around with a pair of silk running shorts. Where's my white singlet? It hasn't come past for ages. There's a hankie. That's all I can see in my tub, one soggy hankie. There's an orgy going on in the next machine. Men's overalls, a lace camisole, all soaking and steaming together. Someone stop this. There are children in here. This machine should have an 'X' rating. Why don't they have single's laundromats? Give me back my clothes, I haven't the courage for the dryers!

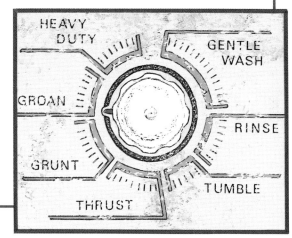

- No Drying Only
- No Pets
- No Sitting By Yourself Reflecting On The
   Misery Of The Human Condition.

PHONE CALL NO. 1
YOUR MUM

Oh darling, it's such bad luck for you. I know how much you wanted this one to work out. Well, never mind, I suppose special people have to try just that little bit harder to find someone just as special. Of course it's the money she was attracted to. I don't want to say 'I told you so', but remember what I said. These women, they'll go for the money every time. You don't want to be tangled up with a woman like her, you'll find someone to love *you*. Bankruptcy won't mean a thing. It'll be you that counts, the real you, not some rubbish in the newspaper, not someone called 'the accused'. That's not the real you, well, it is, I suppose, but you know what I mean.

Yes, I know fifteen years is a long time, sweetheart, but you're lucky to have found out now rather than a bit further down the track. I mean, imagine if you had been hit by that police car outside the jewellers and been turned into a vegetable and found out then that she'd rather be off running all around town with your lawyer. There you'd be, in an iron lung without a leg to stand on. No, you're much better off, now you can just take your time. Yes, fifteen years is a long time darling, you told me already, but you can meet someone really nice. You remember Janice from your old Christian Fellowship Group? For heaven's sake, you don't even notice her ears since she grew her hair long. I told her to bring in her matchbook collection next week. That'll cheer you up, won't it?

Time wounds all heels. JANE ACE

'They were having this affair, right in the house we were all sharing, right under my nose. I found her diary and she had written it all down, as well as all this other intimate stuff about a whole lot of other people. So I took the diary and made photocopies and mailed it to everyone who was mentioned. It really was the talk of the town for a while there.'

HELEN, 26. CHEMIST.

'He left me for this woman who was tall and wore cowboy boots. He's only a small man and the sight of the two of them together was hilarious. Everybody in his office used to laugh behind his back. He'd left this pair of boots behind in the cupboard at home so I took them to the shoe repairer and had the heels raised. Then I painted them with silver stars. I had them delivered to his office in the middle of the staff Christmas party. This mysterious package done up with ribbon arrived and he tore off the wrapping and the boots fell out. Well, everyone in the whole office screamed laughing and he ran outside and threw them in a hedge. People still talk about it and I'm glad I did it. They split up not long after, but I didn't take him back.'

PATRICIA, 39. MOTHER OF TWO.

'Someone told me you can put battery acid in a waterpistol and write all sorts of messages on the furniture. You wouldn't even know it was there until a few days or weeks later when the message began to eat into the upholstery. I would have loved to have done it to her gold drapes in the bedroom. She would have been sitting up in bed with him watching the message appear, like witchcraft. I didn't do it, but I used to sit and think a lot about the words I would have written.'

TIM, 33. WRITER.

My darling,

The time we spent together was so precious to me. I will never forget it. You taught me more about love than I ever thought was possible. But now our time together is over. They say if you love someone you should set them free. You are free.

Grab life, my darling, take it with both hands and squeeze all the happiness you can from it.

I will always be here for you.

I love you. XXXXX

Sweetheart,

I thought I'd better write. I've been ringing and you're never home these days. Caught up in a mad social whirl, eh? It would be great to get together over dinner some time. There's still some things here, records, kitchen stuff. How are you getting along without them? I guess you are getting into the spartan bachelor life.

It seems tacky to have to bring this up in a letter, but there's a few financial matters to sort out. Nothing urgent.

I'm fine, one day seems somehow to drag me into the next.

I miss you.

Robert,

I don't suppose there's much point in sending this to your flat, since everyone tells me you've all but moved in with Sandra. No wonder you didn't need the records and kitchen stuff! Do you still want them? If you do, ring me and come over. Maybe I can cook something. I had a call from the Tax Department the other day. We really should get the return on the company sorted out.

Everyone says Sandra's a nice girl. I'm glad you are happy. Really.

How about giving me a call sometime?

Lots of love.

Dear Robert (Personal)

I've marked this letter 'personal' because I didn't want Sandra to open it. That's what fiancées do, isn't it? It's about time you came and got this stuff because it's cluttering up the cupboard. If you don't want the records I'll give them away. I really can't imagine who'd want an entire set of Jethro Tull records anyway. I'm sure if you took them home it would wreck your image with sophisticated Sandra.

I've got the Tax Department on my back about these returns, Robert, and we must get them done. I have to hear from you by the end of this financial year.

So, when's the wedding? Funny how a man who 'doesn't believe in marriage' can ditch lifelong principles in a matter of months.

PS: I've bought some 'His and Hers' kitchen-sink plugs as a present.

My dear Sandra,

I'm sure Robert has told you all about me. So many folk around town have told me all about you. What an exotic life you have led, you must be relieved to be settling down at last.

I'm glad to hear Robert has finally found someone to marry him. Of course it was something he always talked about when we were together, but I have always been such a free spirit.

One thing to remember: although you are legally entitled to half his property, you are also legally liable for half his debts. Something to think about for the future. Best wishes.

PS: Hope you liked the plugs.

Robert,

While you were away on your honeymoon I decided to see the accountant to sort out the company records. I just didn't feel it fair to worry you with financial details during this special time.

You will recall of course that while I was acting as unpaid general manager/secretary/telephonist/tea lady for the company I put the house in my name for tax purposes. No doubt you will recall saying: 'It doesn't matter whose name the house is in, as long as we are happy'. I'm now extremely happy to be able to tell you that the house sold for a record price of $480,000. I now enclose, with deductions, your share of the proceeds:

Income received $240,000

Less:

Wages general manager	3 years at $28,000 per annum	$84,000.00
Wages secretary	3 years at $19,000 per annum	$57,000.00
Wages telephonist	3 years at $17,000 per annum	$51,000.00
Wages tea lady	3 years at $12,000 per annum	$36,000.00
Adult education computer re-training course		$6,000.00
30 therapy sessions at $100 per session		$3,000.00
Two weeks detoxification health clinic		$1,490.00
Kleenex tissues, 500 boxes at $1.50 each		$750.00
Misc. household bills		$677.00
Rubbish removal		$80.00
Kitchen sink plugs		$2.50

Total: $239,999.50

Please find a cheque enclosed for fifty cents, the full amount owing to you. Yours sincerely.

PS: I sent the kitchenware to a women's refuge. Just thinking of Sandra's future, you understand.

PPS: Hope the sunshine in Tahiti cleared up the eczema on your back.

'He'd been waiting for years and years to get into the Melbourne Cricket Club . . . the real holy of holies. He used to dream about sitting up there with the snobs, drinking Chablis and feeling like he'd really made it. When his membership finally came through I wrote back and told them he was dead. Which was sort of true in a way.'

KAREN, 29. SECRETARY

PHONE CALL NO. 16
YOUR DAD

Well, how's my girl then and to what do I owe this unexpected pleasure? Who? Robert? Which one was he? Oh, the tall chap who was the computer programmer? Quantity surveyor, that's right. Well he was a really lovely chap, darling. Oh, I am sorry to hear that, poppet, really sorry, you quite liked him didn't you? Five years. That's quite a while, isn't it? For goodness sake, sweetheart, you don't want to let it get you down, you're doing so well at work at the moment, you want to get out and enjoy the single life while you can, before you find yourself tied down like your poor old Dad, eh? A gorgeous thing like you, you'll have to fight the blokes off with a stick. Come on . . . that's enough of that self-pitying nonsense. More importantly, how's that car of yours going?

'I filled the bed with food. I pulled back the doona and piled in baked beans, jam, chutney, peanut butter, eggs, sugar, flour . . . everything I could find in the kitchen. Then I remade the bed. It would have been great if she had come home and jumped straight into bed, but she smelt it first because she didn't come home for a few days. I know it's not very original but it was the best I could come up with.'

DAVE, 18. STUDENT.

RECIPES FOR ONE

DEATH BY CHOCOLATE
Place Tim Tams, Freddo Frogs, cooking chocolate, leftover Easter Egg and Coco Pops in food processor. Liquidise. Inject into major artery. Goes well with late-night romantic movies.

POTATO CHIP CRUMBLE
Take two large packets of barbeque, chicken or salt-and-vinegar chips to bed. Eat chips. Throw cellophane packs on floor. Sleep in crumbs. Twisties, Cheezels, Burger Rings or Potato Straws may be substituted when chips unavailable.

TIPSY VEGETARIAN SALAD
Gather healthy salad vegetables on kitchen bench. Play with sharp knife, drink bottle of vodka and think about life. Collapse on kitchen floor. A good recipe for the diet conscious.

PASSIONFRUIT PAVLOVA
Bake and dress pavlova to your favourite recipe. Invite Ex to dinner. Wait by front door with pavlova. Sure to be a hit!

FAST FOOD FIESTA
Take telephone out from under doona cover. Ring Dial-A-Pizza. A tempting, quick and easy solution for the bed-ridden and convalescents.

LEFTOVER MEDLEY
Top a cold slice of pizza with scrapings of last night's spaghetti out of foil container. Fail to find matches. Serve cold with dregs of port bottle. A great dish for when the telephone has been disconnected.

OLIVE DIP
Pour half bottle of virgin olive oil into bath. Light candles. Listen to Leonard Cohen cassette. Slit wrists optional.

Friends believe they can tell a lot about the state of your love life by looking at the way you dress or the hours and company you keep. Your mother thinks she can tell by the amount of times you ring her up. Your boss thinks the number of typing mistakes you make is a clue. But this isn't true. The person who knows most about your love life is Mr Kelvinator.

For example, if you look into a refrigerator and see a bottle of vodka in the freezer and a bottle of nail polish in the cheese compartment, what does this tell you about its owner? It tells you that the single woman who lives here is very likely to come home tired and emotional and skoll the bottle of 'Passion Flame', then try to paint her fingernails with Stolichnaya.

The single man's freezer can't be explored because it will usually be stuck together with the remnants of a can of beer which exploded the night before. Even if you could get it open you would find out all sorts of things you didn't really want to know—like how baked beans can sustain alien life-forms and butter really does go black in the end.

Single people also have Beroccas in where the eggs go. They understand that you musn't let Beroccas go off. There are vitamins in them and fresh food is important in the diet.

But the next stage in the life cycle of the fridge is an exotic feast. There is a new lover and suddenly the shelves are full of sex aids: French champagne, strawberries, honey, fresh eggs . . . Dairy Whip.

The blindingly infatuated couple have seen the steamy fridge scene in *9½ weeks* and know this is real love because they don't even stop to think how they are going to clean the three metre strawberry omelette off the floor in the morning.

Not a moment too soon the happy couple create a nest together and the fridge is a testament to the love they share. The shelves groan seductively with fresh vegetables from the market, home-made jam, two lamb chops nestling together in a meaty heart. When the door of the fridge is opened the light doesn't just switch on, it positively glows.

Everything seems perfect, then one day the bulb blows. There are things in the dark recesses of the shelves the couple never thought they'd see. Leftovers. Someone didn't come home last night. A half-eaten casserole covered in plastic wrap with a note: 'You know how to work the microwave, heat this up yourself.' Strawberries are out of season and the jam's gone mouldy.

Then, sadly, it's back to a fridge for one. Its owner keeps buying food for two, hoping, hoping, but all that's left is a crisper full of compost. Every now and then the single person will stand in front of the fridge to reminisce about lost loves. The newly replaced bulb burning brightly on the cool steel shelves. And if they look very carefully they may find, down behind the drip tray, one lone limp carrot, or two sad oranges, and think: 'Hey, maybe eating out isn't so bad after all.'

'Well, I knew he was going to be away a few weeks on business so I got into his flat and soaked the carpet, the furniture, his clothes, and the bed—especially the bed—with water. Then I sowed watercress seeds everywhere and turned the central heating up full. Apparently it was about three inches high when he got back.'

SANDRA, 24. STOCKBROKER.

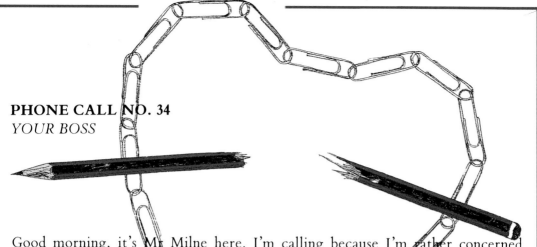

PHONE CALL NO. 34
YOUR BOSS

Good morning, it's Mr Milne here. I'm calling because I'm rather concerned that we haven't seen much of you lately, here at the office. Yes, Mrs Rosenberg tells me you've had doctors' certificates, but they seem to be a bit vague, and, quite frankly, not serious enough to really be keeping you away from work all this time. Well, I don't know how easy it will be for you to catch up. The quality of your work is really starting to slide too, and you can't expect your workmates to carry the load for you. I mean we were badly shorthanded at the stocktake. Is it anything personal? Can I help? Mrs Rosenberg tells me she found you sharpening a pile of ball point pens the other day and on Friday she asked for a contribution to Sally's engagement present and you ran off in tears and locked yourself in the stationery cabinet. You realise I'll have to dock your pay for the hire of the oxywelding equipment. Perhaps you'd better tell me all about it. Mmm, yes, I see, I understand, of course, absolutely, by yourself, that must be hard for you. Well, I'm here to help, you know that. All my lovely ladies here at the office know that. No, please, call me Reg. I'll tell you what, I've got a conference in New Zealand coming up soon—Market Systems Analysis in the Footwear Industry, Asia-Pacific Region. It should really be a lot of fun, we had a ball last year, no pun intended, ha ha. Why don't you come with me as my 'personal assistant'? It'll be a great opportunity for you to really see the high rollers in action and then we can rock the night away in swinging Auckland. Whaddya say? Yes, well, given that sort of attitude and your work record lately I think the best thing would be to see Mrs Rosenberg in the morning and pick up your severance pay. Good morning.

8 pm That's the house. It's smaller than I'd imagined. Weatherboard, single storey, pretty ordinary street. He can't be doing that well. Not much of a 'love nest'. I wonder if there's a yard out the back, a yard where they sit and drink wine, eat breakfast. I'm not going to stay. I've seen the place.

8.30pm Maybe she's not coming. She's found something better to do. She's stood him up. He'll be sitting there waiting and she won't arrive. I'll leave. That's all I needed to know. So they don't spend every night together. I knew it.

9pm Oh my God, here she comes. Duck! Can she see the car? She hasn't noticed the car. She looks wonderful. That's a new dress, she looks thinner. She's got a bag with her. What's in the bag? Lingerie? Not that black lace number I bought her for Christmas. She wouldn't wear that with anyone else, would she? Groceries. She's got wine in there. No, champagne, her favourite. They'll make supper together, music playing, cold glasses of champagne, kisses in the kitchen. We used to kiss in the kitchen. He's opening the door. He looks fat and old. She's walked straight in. No cuddles at the front door. They don't want people to know. Hiding from the neighbours. We used to cuddle at the door every night. Now I'm going. I've got better things to do than sit here night after night watching this tawdry liaison. They don't go out. Too ashamed to be seen in public.

9.10pm Wait a minute. The light's gone on in that end room. What room would that be? Wouldn't be the kitchen, right down the end there. Would it? The kitchen's right down one end at the Palace of Versailles, I read that somewhere. But this isn't Versailles, not by a long chalk. This is a dump. I hate this place. How could she lower herself? I always thought she had a bit of class, in a funny kind of way. I hate this, I'm leaving.

9.12pm Now the other light has gone off. Now they're in that end room. Shit. Maybe it's the toilet. But they wouldn't both be in there! Maybe she's gone to the toilet and he's . . . sitting in the dark. What the hell is on his mind, that's what I'd like to know! I do know. I know what's on his mind. He's sitting there in the dark feeling horny. He's gonna spring it on her the second she comes out of the . . .

9.13pm It's all dark! She doesn't know what she's gotten herself into. She's an innocent really. She wouldn't know a pervert if she saw one. She's bitten off more than she can chew. She doesn't like it with the light off. We never used to 'turn the light off'! What a fifties idea. This guy's a creep. You'd have to do it in the dark with him, he's so ugly. And old. I bet she's changed her mind but she can't get away. He's probably tied her up. He'd HAVE to.

9.15pm I used to fantasise about tying her up.

9.20pm Anyway, it's none of my business. It's all dark. I can't see anything. What is there to see, anyhow? But it's none of my business, really. I'm going. She made her bed, now she can lie in it. I'm going home so I can be there when she rings up to tell me what a bad time she's had and how it was all a terrible mistake and all her fault and I told her so.

9.30pm OK, I'm off. This is ridiculous. I've been hanging around here long enough. They've been at it for . . . what? Fifteen minutes? He probably came fourteen minutes ago. Of course, I could be wrong. They could be watching TV somewhere. I can't see all of the place from here. I can't see the back. If I could see the back, I'd know then. Once and for all. I'll never come back here again.

9.32pm Shit, it's cold. Wish I'd worn a jacket. Or a balaclava. Brrr! I'll just take a quick look. Over the side fence. Doesn't look as if anyone's home next door. If I just nick down their drive, look over the fence, and piss off. Wouldn't want people to get the wrong idea.

9.35pm I'm trespassing. I'm actually trespassing! Don't worry, it's OK. I'm only perving. It's a crime of passion. It's not even a crime, it's a misdemeanour of passion. Bugger, I can't see a thing. Why has he got all those fucking bushes? Trying to hide something, no doubt. Creep. Too lazy to cut them back. Thinks they look good there, I suppose. Well, they look shithouse. They're the worst looking . . .

9.37pm Shit, the Police! I'd know that blue light anywhere. Lie low, you'll never explain it. They're checking out the car.

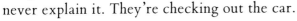
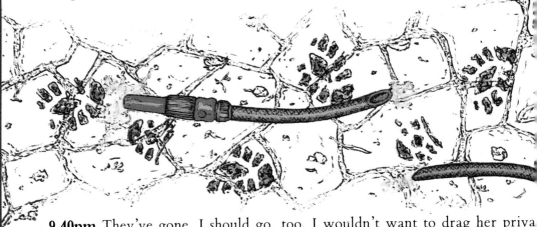

9.40pm They've gone. I should go, too. I wouldn't want to drag her priva life through the courts. She deserves it, though. No jury would convict m that's for sure. Convict me of what? I haven't done a thing. I'm clean. Whi is more than I can say for HER! I could see the back of the house fro up there, if I could just ease myself up this trellis or whatever it is. OUC What the . . . who leaves a pile of bricks in a place like this? I could bre my neck. Inconsiderate bastard.

9.45pm No lights. What's that sound? I can hardly catch . . . it's a record. It's . . . who is it? I know that voice. It's some jazz singer. Some sexy, late-night-rendezvous-type jazz singer, crooning. What a cheap trick! No, it's HER! She's tied up with a handkerchief over her face and she's trying to call for help! She's in pain! She's moaning! She's moaning!

9.50pm Oh God, oh God, oh God. This is the pits. She must feel so cheap.

9.55pm I don't know why I'm on the roof. It's bloody cold up here. I'll stay here for a while, I think. It's dark, I'm going to kill myself trying to get down. I'm not ready for that yet. Not quite. I'm happy up here. It's cosy in an exposed kind of way. I think I've been happier up here than any other place on earth. I'll just sit here for a long time. What does she care? No-one's going to stop me. I'm not, you know, dangerous or anything. I don't want to hurt anybody. I wouldn't hurt a fly.

10.05pm I'll kill him. I'll slip a sharp knife right through his fat guts.

10.35pm I'm really cold now. Is she staying the whole night or what? That fucking wind goes right through you. Oops, shit, those bloody bricks . . .

POLICE REPORT

At 21.33 hours on the evening of Friday, March 26, I received a call from a Mr Winton, 32 Roseland Street, Parkdale, regarding a yellow Torana parked in the front of his residence. Mr Winton informed me that the car had been parked in the vicinity of his residence every evening for the past month.

Officer Cartland and myself inspected the vehicle and found it empty, with the keys still in the ignition. We found an empty bottle of Johnny Walker Black Label on the passenger seat and from the smell inside the car it appeared the contents had recently been consumed. We could see no-one within the immediate vicinity of the car.

At 22.40 hours I received another call from Mr Winton to say that a house brick had been thrown through the rear-bedroom window of his residence.

Officer Cartland and myself approached the rear of the residence and heard a male voice say 'I will kill you, you fat, old bastard'. The voice sounded both agitated and intoxicated and appeared to be coming from the roof of the residence.

On further investigation we discovered a Caucasian male, whom we later identified as Graham Alan Scott, 42 years, of 153 Victoria Road, Smithgate.

Both Officer Cartland and myself appealed to the suspect to come down from the roof and were assaulted with an offensive weapon, namely, one housebrick.

Scott was eventually taken into custody with the assistance of members of the Tactical Response Group, the Dog Squad and a high-pressure fire hose supplied by the Metropolitan Fire Brigade.

Things that love night love not such nights as these. WILLIAM SHAKESPEARE. *KING LEAR.*

PHONE CALL NO. 56
THE EX's GIRLFRIEND

Oh hi, it's me, Karen. I'm just so sorry to hear about you and Jane. Really. Oh yeah, I saw her last night. Well, I didn't get to talk to her much, she was racing out the door. But the main thing is, how are you? You poor thing. I bet you are, you poor darling. Well, we were all shocked, I mean I just can't understand how she could let a man like you slip through her fingers. Jane? Oh a party I think, some people from the gym were having some kind of get-together, apparently. Are you eating OK? Look, you can't just drink yourself into oblivion, you've got to eat properly. I'm not really sure, she was in such a hurry. Well, yeah, I suppose he'll be there, he's been taking aerobics classes for quite a while now. But you've just got to get your mind off Jane. Maybe I should come over and cook something for you. You've always really liked my cooking, haven't you? Look you are the one I'm worried about, I know Jane's a good friend of mine and everything, but she'll just bounce back. I mean with the amount of time she's been spending at the gym recently she's certainly fit enough. She's so amazing Jane, I mean I just can't keep up with her. You know me, I'd much rather lounge around in bed all day. She looks fantastic, I know but, to tell you the truth, I've always thought she was a teeny bit obsessive. Some women just don't know how to relax and really let themselves go with a man. Love isn't just some athletic sexual marathon, it can also be great food, wine, books and cosy nights at home. Don't you think?

I'll be over in half an hour.

HIS

Compact disc player
Tupperware containers (egg blue)
parsley, sage, rosemary, thyme
one set Wiltshire 'Eternity' knives
one duck feather doona (fake)
tent (sleeps two)
television (with coathanger)
Encyclopedia Britannica A-K
Photographs Paris, Sept 88
Karen, Richard, Louis
Ted and Ann (Tues, Thurs, Sat)
Cafe La Greque, Bayside Cinema
right half Victorian terrace house
legal rights
lawyers' bills
severe depression
insomnia

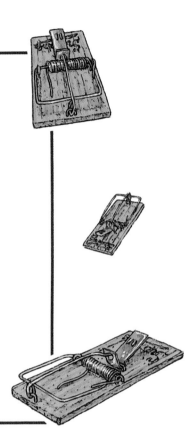

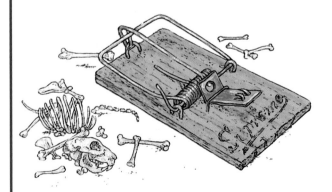

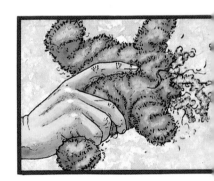

HERS

Compact discs
Tupperware lids (pale pink)
coriander, turmeric, cloves, saffron
one set Wilshire 'Eternity' forks
one doona cover (soiled)
guyropes (one missing)
video recorder (Beta)
Encyclopedia Britannica L-Z
Photographs QLD, June 89
Phillip, Angela, Jean
Ted and Ann (Mon, Wed, Fri)
Chez Lorraine, Plaza City Twin
left half Victorian terrace house
moral high ground
lawyers' bills
acute paranoia
headaches

Folk who live to be 100 years old are often asked the secret of their longevity. 'Moderation in all things, my dear', they reply. And those who want to live to be 100 are reminded to cut down on alcohol, sweets and fats, to drag their jogging shoes from the bottom of the cupboard.

Moderation? Ha!

The best, most blissful thing about being brokenhearted is that you don't give a fuck if you wake up dead tomorrow. The way you feel, a month in intensive care with liver failure sounds like fun; lapsing into a coma pure joy.

Yes it's binge time, time to wreck your health. Your spirits are devastated. Why not have a body to match? Give the addiction of your choice a run for its money. Gain fifteen kilos or become anorexic—who gives a stuff if your good clothes don't fit. Tracksuits always expand or contract to cover available body surface. You're never going to have sex with anyone again, so who cares? Become a hopeless drunk. Right now you've got the best excuse in the world. Tell people it's a new form of Jungian therapy—you took a look at the dark side of the self and decided it needed a few strong drinks to lighten up. Take all the drugs you always wanted but couldn't find a reasonable excuse for. Walk the streets at night even if it's only to the corner shop for a soft pack of Marlboro. Overdraw your bank account. Stick things up your nose until your sinuses collapse and mix with the sort of wasted no-hopers you find in Sam Shepard plays. Throw a party—one of those parties where you throw down sawdust and make sure your ambulance subscription is paid up. Watching relationships around you break up and reform like bacteria will make you feel much better. Spend most of the evening in the bathroom with a razor blade while people try to talk you out of it.

Any of these forms of behaviour is a perfectly acceptable means of manifesting pain and extracting enormous amounts of alarmed attention from friends and family as well as causing maximum guilt for the Ex. Well, think of the remaining option: 'Maybe having a broken heart agrees with you, you're certainly looking terrific these days.' Remember, checking into the Betty Ford Clinic carries enormous social cachet in this enlightened era and, if you do a really good job on this one, you could end up on *60 Minutes*.

THE 'DOUBLE YOUR OWN BODYWEIGHT IN A WEEK' DIET.

The hole in your self-esteem is a bottomless pit. You are now going to tip food into it so it fills up and you feel better. Think of the way City Councils fill quarries with millions of tonnes of household garbage and then plant attractive shrubs on the surface: now you have a useful mental image to work with.

Anything labelled 'enriched', 'full', 'family size' or 'now with added' which doesn't need to be plugged in, repaired or disposed of thoughtfully, you can eat. Simply: a) remove wrapper b) insert in mouth.

THE 'OH MY GOD, ARE YOU OK?' DIET.

This regime is for those who would rather starve their self-esteem to death. It's especially good for women who still think fainting spells are attractive and believe in the maxim: 'You can never be too thin or too rich'. Wrong. If Karen Carpenter had been in a lower income bracket she would still be alive today.

If you can sustain your body on a packet of jelly beans for a week, you're well on the way with this diet. A word or two of warning: watch out for grates in footpaths, bath plugholes and cracks in the back of sofas.

THE 'GOVERNMENT HEALTH WARNING' DIET.

Anything which has been the subject of a pamphlet written by a Government health agency can be consumed in this 'instant result' diet. The staples are high tar cigarettes, any spirits over forty per cent alcohol by volume, and any substance which will not make it through customs without attracting the attention of a sniffer dog. You can forget kitchen mess with this one, but it does have its drawbacks. Maintaining credit lines with Bolivian drug cartels has never been cheap and you also run an extremely high risk of thinking you are Charles Bukowski and writing something incredibly self-indulgent.

*'We'd bought this love seat at this antique shop up the country. It
was red velvet, pretty shabby looking but we used to sit in it and
drink champagne and read poetry, you know, all the romantic stuff.
Anyway when she left me I chopped it up with an axe. It felt
really good.'*

GREG, 24. ACTOR.

PHONE CALL NO. 74
YOUR GOOD FRIEND

How are you? I just heard from Sarah everyone's talking about it. So you finally
got rid of him then. Congratulations! I mean, really, none of us could believe
how long you put up with the whole situation with him and Maria. It must
have been so humiliating when you finally found out. Well, how could we
tell you? We were just hoping he would have the guts to own up. What a
bastard! You know Maria is just as upset as you . . . the poor thing. Honestly
it's been so bizarre for all of us. Remember the cocktail party for Barry's going
away. Well, I mean, when we realised that all three of you were going to
 be in the same room together! As it was Maria
walked in about ten minutes after you two had
left and everyone in the whole room just
breathedthe hugest sigh of relief. Actually it's
pretty funny if you think about it. No, I suppose
it isn't really. But I mean, honestly, couldn't you
see what he was up to? I mean he even tried
it on on me. You knew that, didn't you? Well,
why would I tell you, it was such a pathetic
attempt, he's such a creep I just didn't take him seriously. Oh hang on, I've got
to go, Kristin has just walked in and she'll just die when she hears. See ya!

*'Women generally go for cutting up his clothes, but I reckon the
best revenge on her would be to replace all the clothes in her
wardrobe with identical items two sizes smaller. Wouldn't that
send her crazy! I wish I could have afforded that one.'*

CAMERON, 45. TEACHER.

When you are brokenhearted hairdressing salons begin to have an irrational appeal. Your poor demented brain tells you that an expensive and outrageous haircut might be just the ticket to a new you and a new life. If you have straight hair you begin to fantasise about a ravishing tumble of pre-Raphaelite curls. Cool brunettes long for re-birth as fiery redheads. Smooth blondes want black spikes. Stop! You must see your urge to have your hair cut as a deep desire to reinforce your present feelings of worthlessness. What happened to Samson when he had his locks lopped? That's right. The roof fell on his head.

Be warned, a hairdressing salon is no place to find balm for the savaged soul. This place is an unholy chamber of horrors . . . flashing scissors, scourging bleach, hissing metal tongs, scalding water and noxious sprays. Think of that cape to keep the hair off your clothes as a thinly disguised straightjacket. See your hairdresser as a master torturer who wants to break your already fragile spirit.

Would you consider a visit to the dentist a marvellous, restorative indulgence? Of course you wouldn't. Similarly, an appointment with the hairdresser only leads to pain and a feeling of violation. Have you noticed that hairdressing salons, with their minimalist chrome, hard spotlights and mirrors, are looking more than ever like dentists' rooms? Meanwhile dentists' rooms are looking more like old-fashioned hairdressing salons with comforting potted plants, rustic prints and piped music.

What we need now is an anaesthetic for a haircut.

A visit to the hairdresser is a study in pyschological warfare. You approach the surly but immaculately coiffed young woman behind the counter who breaks an interminable telephone conversation with her boyfriend to glare at you.

'I'm sorry, Carol can't do your hair today, but Bluey will be looking after you. He's just been working on a station.'

'Oh . . . television station?'

'No . . . sheep.'

You take your place in the reception room to flip through back issues of fashion magazines. You look up your horoscope from March 1982 trying to remember if that month really was a good one for 'tall, dark strangers' and you know it wasn't—because your whole life hasn't been. Every now and then you look up at people leaving with their new haircuts and think: 'My God, did they ask for that!'

You laugh too soon, because just when you are having second thoughts you are dragged to the washbasin and dumped in an anatomically impossible chair. Your spinal cord is asked to compensate for the design faults in this apparatus.

'Lean back, lean back, just a bit further,' says the sorcerer's apprentice who, when he hears the 'crack', will be satisfied. Who designed these chairs? Mr Gumby the Plasticene Man?

In most salons your hair is washed by the cutest young apprentice on the premises, who, while running his fingers sensually through your locks, grinds his crotch into the side of your neck. There is nothing you can do about this exquisite torture without drawing the attention of the authorities.

The apprentice chats amiably while applying the Chinese water torture with frightening dexterity. You can't hear a thing . . . water bubbles in your ears and pours down the back of your neck. What he's telling you translates as something like, 'My mother', gurgle, gurgle, 'a duck', dribble, splash, 'three Hare Krishnas in a Volvo'.

You lean back, agreeing and smiling inanely, 'Oh yes, you're quite right there, I couldn't agree more'. You have no idea what you've just agreed to, but it's bound to be ugly. The apprentice finishes off by removing most of your distinguishing facial features with a towel and handing you a business card for a leather and rubber garment manufacturer with his telephone number written on the back.

Then, just at the psychological moment, in walks Bluey. He's six-foot-four, wearing snowy moleskin jeans, RM Williams boots, navy singlet with an 'I love Jack Thompson' tattoo on his forearm and he's rolling a 'Tally Ho' in one hand. He looks at you and says, 'Gidday love, who done your hair last?'.

You think, 'My God, either this bloke is out of the crowd scene of *Conan The Barbarian* or someone's given a New South Wales shearer the power of speech.' Either way you pray it's not the crutching season.

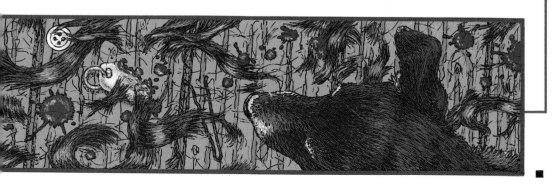

Now is the time for you to say how you want your hair done. All rational thought leaves you.

'Ummm, er, what I had in mind was ummm, something Kylie-Peter Garrett-ish.

'What I thought we could do was . . . just cut the back into a shortish kind of thing, but leave the top because I'm trying to grow that bit . . . I just want to be able to get out of the shower and leave it . . . but I'd like to be able to put it up sometimes . . . maybe put some hair gel into it . . . cut it around the front, but not in a fringe because that doesn't suit me . . . maybe a perm but I just mostly want it to look natural . . . just like this woman in the magazine . . . except she's blonde and got cheekbones.'

And this is where you completely give up and utter those fatal words, 'Look, I'll leave it up to you.'

These are exactly the words Bluey is waiting to hear. He's just back from Berlin where he's seen an anti-gravity, reverse-layered mohawk and he's dying to try it out on someone.

And while you vainly try to struggle out of the straightjacket, Bluey grabs the wide-bodied shearing comb and takes a good ten inches of hair and an inch of lobe off one side.

The frightening thing is, he has to cut the other side to match.

Now it's time for your colour. Your colour is always done by a recent school-leaver, who majored in finger painting and Rockabilly, wearing a T-shirt which gives you acid flashbacks to the early seventies.

She looks at you and says, 'Your hair's just sitting there. It's not really saying anything'.

Your hair replies, 'Yes I am, lean closer. Help! Help! Get me out of here!'

'You know what would look good on you? Something hard-edged yet feminine, come-hither yet somehow stand-offish. Something . . .'

'Chestnut?'

'No, orange.'

'Subtle?'

'No, fluorescent.'

She covers your head with bits of pipe-cleaner and silver foil so you look like that creature out of *Alien*. She does this close to the window so people passing by can watch. This is a cheap form of street theatre.

Then she wheels out this barrel full of noxious, seeping stuff which she handles wearing a full-face mask with a pair of long-handled tongs. She pours it onto your head through a lead-lined funnel.

The film crew from *60 Minutes* arrives and your hair's sizzling, there's smoke rising and you realise, 'It's orange all right . . . it's AGENT ORANGE!'.

The sound of a million choppers swarms out of a low-rising Asian sun . . . The Ride of the Valkyries blasts through your toxic scalp. 'You smell that, you smell that! That's hair dye son, I love the smell of hair dye in the morning.'

'Shit, Saigon . . ., I was still in Saigon.'

You get the picture . . . don't get your hair cut. Getting your hair cut to mend a broken heart is about as useful as invading Indochina to secure world peace.

Hey! We're gonna win this war, kiddo!

(Just as gas masks have become a must-have accessory for surviving modern warfare, wigs can get you through the worst. You'll look exotic and won't have to worry about them sliding off in moments of unbridled passion.)

Any moment now you will be hit by an overwhelming urge to indulge in a monumental shopping spree. You want things that sparkle, rustle, crackle, shine and rattle. Things that look new, feel soft, smell beautiful and sound wonderful.

You may dismiss this urge as a primitive desire for self-gratification in the face of a problem which requires a more measured response. Nothing could be further from the truth. Shopping is exactly what you need, and lots of it.

You might rationalise that the only reason you want to go shopping is to replace the warm and pampered feeling you get after particularly good sex. Shopping is not a replacement for sex, shopping is BETTER than sex. Any beast of the field or bird of the air can do sex. Let's face it, sex is relatively easy for all living species, but the ability to shop is what separates human beings from their little friends in the animal kingdom.

Some beasts do make primitive attempts at shopping—the Satin Bower Bird is much admired for its habit of collecting small pieces of blue bric a brac to adorn its boudoir—but if there are no bits of blue about the bird cannot even grasp the simple concept of 'red'. Certainly the idea of hunting about for something in a mottled beige toning to match with the imported Italian twigs and designer straw is way beyond the little featherbrain's capabilities.

So, feel proud. When human beings shop they are displaying all the skills which put the species at the top of the evolutionary ladder. If you are given the choice between an afternoon in the stores or between the sheets, announce loudly: 'What sort of animal do you think I am?' Grab your credit card and go!

Shopping is better than sex because:

- Doing it by yourself is usually much more gratifying than doing it with someone else.
- You can have your mother along if you get lonely.
- You get to keep your clothes on.
- It doesn't muck up your hair.
- The only health risks are sore feet or credit card elbow.
- You can have a Norgen Vaaz while you're doing it and not make a mess.
- If your ex-lover turns up you can pretend you haven't seen him or her.
- You can stop halfway for a cappuccino and a French pastry.
- You don't have to fake having a good time. (E.g., you don't have to pretend you are in Harrods when you are in K-Mart.)
- There's something nice to keep at the end which is not a baby.

When do I go?

The only time for a therapeutic shopping trip is on a Friday when all the wage slaves are still at work. Tell your boss you have a family funeral to attend. The more clandestine the expedition the greater the gratification. Take the day, take a taxi, take liberties and plan to shop till you drop.

Where do I go?

Remember that as a shopper you are now at the centre of the retailing universe. Every shop in the world has its doors thrown open to you. That $35,000 Chinchilla coat only exists because you might buy it. Solid gold cufflinks are on display for you alone.

Never mind if you are wearing sunglasses held together with sticky tape and carrying a bag of cat meat, you could be an eccentric millionaire who just chooses to dress like a greengrocer.

March straight into the boutique where that anorexic blonde with plastic fingernails and an IQ smaller than her hip measurement reigns as queen. Demand to try on the black chiffon evening dress with the real jet beads, then tell her you just remembered you have one exactly the same at home. Tell the man with the nasty moustache to ring head office because you want a blue, pure cashmere jumper the same shade as your eyes.

Take a Porsche for a test drive. Ask to listen to all of La Traviata before you buy the CD. Taste a bit of every cheese in the cabinet. Steal a cherry macaroon from the lolly counter. Test all the fountain pens in the shop. Ask them to hold the diamond necklace until you get back from the bank.

What do I buy?

Something ridiculous that you've always wanted, don't need and can barely afford.

Avoid kitchen utensils, hardware items, office equipment, household cleaners, weapons, and, most especially, a little something for your ex-lover that you saw and know he or she would just adore. This is your shopping day, a time to be absolutely selfish.

Good bets are anything edible, fragile, fragrant, crushable or sticky.

What then?

Take everything home, unwrap all the parcels, throw the recyclable tissue paper and bio-degradable plastic bags around the room and lie in the middle. Examine each item lovingly and congratulate yourself on your superb taste. If you've bought things to wear, try them on and parade around in front of the mirror. If you've bought things to listen to, play them as loud as you want. Carefully open the last item: an exquisite Belgian chocolate and eat this while cutting up your credit card with a pair of scissors.

Then get really drunk because now you're not only by yourself, you're broke as well.

PHONE CALL NO. 89
THE NEW COUPLE

Hello . . . hello . . . hello . . . who's this? Hello . . . is anyone there? Speak up please. Hello . . . hello . . . I know someone's there. Hello . . . oh, not again. Look, we know it's you. Why are you doing this to us? Nick, it's her again. You know exactly who I mean. I'm sick of this and I want her to stop ringing and this time you'd better tell her yourself because if this keeps happening I'm calling the police. It's four o'clock in the morning, for Christ's sake. Talk to her.

All right, give me the phone. Hello . . . hello . . . what do you want? Come on . . . speak to me. Hello . . . look if you won't talk to me I'm going to hang up . . . I'll hang up! Look, it's been eighteen months now, you can't keep doing this. Are you OK? You haven't taken anything again have you? Have you taken something? Damn. Look I'll have to go over, sweetheart, she could have done anything. I'm sorry, darling, this will be the last time, I promise I'll sort this out once and for all.

Give me the bloody phone. Listen to me you manipulative bitch. Get it through your stupid thick head once and for all. Nick lives with me, he loves me, he is not coming back. He isn't with *you* because he doesn't love *you*. Get your claws out of his back, get out of our lives, get off this phone! Nick, get back into bed! Nick! You bitch! I hate you!

START AGAIN

ADVANTAGES OF BEING BY MYSELF
None.

DISADVANTAGES OF BEING BY MYSELF
I have to get my own drink of water in the middle of the night.
There's no-one to tell me when I'm getting fat.
The bread goes stale before I can eat it all.
There's no-one to laugh at my jokes.
I look like a loser in restaurants.
I have to put the rubbish bins out every time.
There's no-one to tell me when I'm singing off key.
I have to read the road map *and* drive the car.
There's no-one to share secrets with.
The bed is cold and empty.
I have no excuses for not staying for Christmas dinner.
I only have baths to wash myself.
It's costing me double the rent.
I have to pay to get a foot massage.
My friends keep trying to match me with other losers.
There's no-one to kiss the back of my neck.
I have to have sex with strangers.

GO

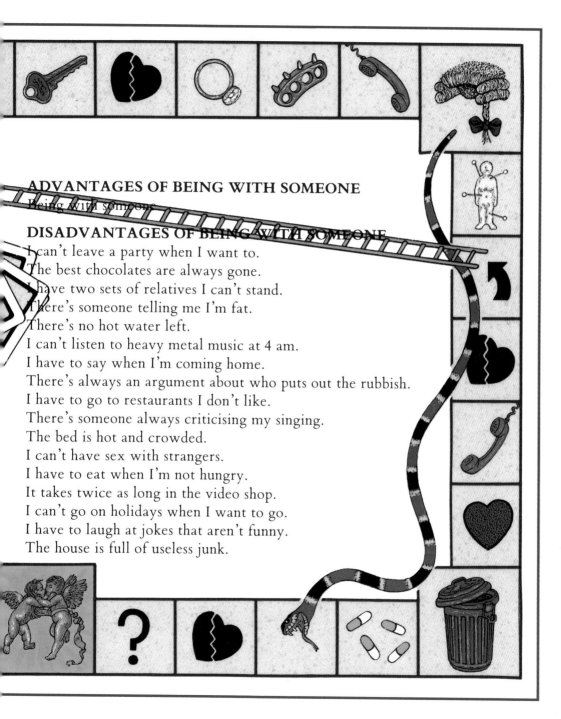

ADVANTAGES OF BEING WITH SOMEONE
Being with someone

DISADVANTAGES OF BEING WITH SOMEONE
I can't leave a party when I want to.
The best chocolates are always gone.
I have two sets of relatives I can't stand.
There's someone telling me I'm fat.
There's no hot water left.
I can't listen to heavy metal music at 4 am.
I have to say when I'm coming home.
There's always an argument about who puts out the rubbish.
I have to go to restaurants I don't like.
There's someone always criticising my singing.
The bed is hot and crowded.
I can't have sex with strangers.
I have to eat when I'm not hungry.
It takes twice as long in the video shop.
I can't go on holidays when I want to go.
I have to laugh at jokes that aren't funny.
The house is full of useless junk.

'He only took a small suitcase so I got the rest of his clothes and put them through the mulcher and then in the compost bin. For months afterwards I would see gold buttons off his best jacket, bits of ties, shirts, trousers. I put the compost around the roses. It was sort of fitting . . . ashes to ashes . . . dust to dust. Honestly the roses never looked better.'

BARBARA, 45. BOUTIQUE OWNER.

PHONE CALL NO. 82
YOUR BEST MATE

Gidday, mate. Yeah, I heard the bad news and the first thing I thought was it's almost exactly the same as what happened to me and Tracey. Just out of the blue, mate, completely unexpected, one minute she was there and the next minute, thin air . . . no explanation. Yeah, well you would feel shithouse, mate . . . if it's anywhere near as bad as what happened to me and Tracey . . . yeah, well that's exactly what Tracey did to me, mate and I said to her, you can't just walk out without talking about it. She reckons I never listen to her, but that's not true, I, . . . yeah, well Tracey did that to me too. See the thing was with us that I didn't realise that Tracey, yeah, well OK, mate, if you have to go . . . yeah, no worries, any time I can help you sort out your problems give us a call . . . that's what friends are for, mate, see when me and Traccy broke up . . .

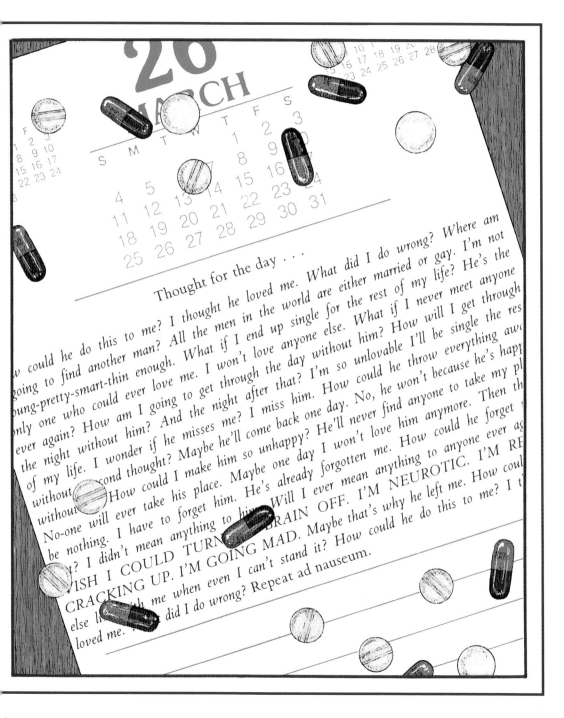

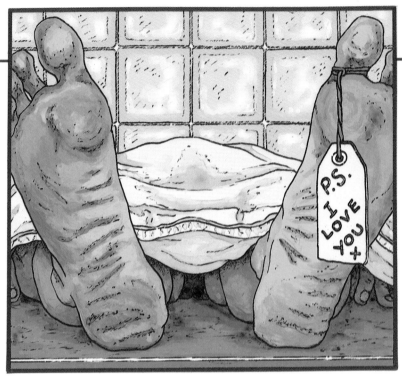

'Is life worth living?' is a question bound to occur to you sooner or later. All too often a resounding 'no' will be the reply. Depending on your sense of the theatric your suicide will either be a brutal event—a team of emergency workers will spend hours cutting your body from the mangled wreck of a high-powered automobile, only to have you pronounced DOA at the casualty unit—or it will be an elegant and poignant affair. A friend will find your body attired in tasteful nightwear slumped on the floor, a bottle of Seconal and a note on the bedside table just out of reach.

But unfortunately real life death doesn't turn out that way. It's just as likely the auto wreck will leave you on crutches, with years to contemplate your failure to pull off The Big One. Or think of Lupe Velez, 'The Mexican Spitfire', the passionate Hollywood movie star of the twenties who planned a gorgeous suicide in her Rodeo Drive hacienda.

She dressed in silver lamé, stuffed her abode with gardenias and tuberoses, and invited two girlfriends to her Last Supper. When they left she downed the Seconals and lay down on her bed surrounded by dozens of glowing candles— a suitably tragic tableau. But the pills didn't mix with the last supper and her maid discovered her body headfirst down the toilet. The credits rolled over a closing scene more sordid than sumptuous.

You might imagine your funeral as your starring role. Grainy black and white. A Gothic church full of sobbing mourners. Mounds of fragrant flowers and melancholic strains from the massed choir as your coffin is borne slowly aloft. It's always a coffin. You are never cremated in funeral fantasies. People can't stand under umbrellas in the rain around a furnace, can they? And besides you need a headstone for people to lie on crying, 'Our lives are meaningless now, why did you leave us!'

There's one other reason why you need a good-looking corpse—if you have to come back and haunt someone you want to be in good shape. You don't want your Ex's new spouse to be able to taunt you with the line, 'Hmm, no wonder he left you, you really let yourself go. You're the most out of condition ghost I've ever seen.' And somehow an eerie cry and clank of chains doesn't have the same impact coming from a small pile of ashes on the hall table.

In your suicide reverie you can see the newspaper headlines as the final extra hits stands all over the City.

HEARTBREAK, DEATH, HORROR, SHOCK

The world was shaken today to learn of the death of . . . . (insert your own name here) in tragic circumstances.

From first reports it appears that . . . . took his/her own life in what friends have described as "the most devastating case of a broken heart ever seen".

Floral tributes have begun to pour in from world leaders. The Dow Jones index plunged a massive 110 points when news of the sad loss hit the trading floor of the New York Stock Exchange. Other world markets are bracing themselves.

The Prime Minister has declared today one of national mourning. ". . . . . was not only a great Australian, but an inspiration to millions. The loss will be keenly felt by everyone forever," the PM said this afternoon.

Federal Authorities have swung into action in an all-out effort to track down . . . . (insert your Ex's name here) who appears to have gone into hiding on hearing the news. "We can only hope that . . . . is found and brought to justice," distraught friends said. If brought to trial and convicted . . . . could face a life sentence of guilt, remorse and solitude.

"We know that's the way . . . . would have wanted it," friends added. (Cont. P. 3)

More reports, world reaction, photographs: middle pages.

World War Three Declared (p. 15)

There's one element missing from this dramatic suicide scenario . . . and that's you.

One scene remains on the cutting-room floor. It's that final sequence where you stand at the cemetery gates to shout triumphantly to your Ex-lover: 'Look what you did to me . . . you made me kill myself!'

If you have thought long and hard about suicide and decide you really must, a few tips on etiquette:

• Always check the spelling in your suicide note. 'I have gorne, life is to trajic' will leave folk reflecting more on the failure of the State education system rather than your sad demise. (You might like to try leaving a number of notes addressed to different

people: your Sixth Form maths teacher, football coach, boss, all your Ex-lovers, etc. This is a good way to ensure your funeral will be impressive in the floral tribute department.) Under no circumstances succumb to the urge to make your suicide note rhyme. There is enough bad poetry in the world as it is. A haiku is an acceptable compromise.

• If you are going to shoot yourself, choose a handgun designed for the job. A heavy-gauge double-barrelled shotgun will leave too much of you behind and you run the risk of ending up in a carpet shampoo advertisement.

• Don't show off. Self-immolation in the City Square may lead people to think you are some sort of religious or political zealot and your passport photograph may end up being worn in the middle of a horrible carved wooden pendant by badly dressed hippies.

• Don't forget that fingernails and hair keep on growing for some time after death, so do spend extra time on personal grooming.

• If you are opting for the carbon monoxide asphyxiation method please use lead-free petrol.

• It is worthwhile taking the extra time to bequeath items to selected family and friends. The bereaved put on a better show if they know there's something to keep at the end and you want to avoid at all costs your Ex ending up with the CD player and your favourite Charlie Mingus discs.

• Try to pull it off in one. If you can't make a decent go of your life try to make your death a success. No-one likes a complete loser.

PHONE CALL NO. 115
THE EX'S MOTHER

Oh, it's just such a rotten shame. I just don't know what's gotten into him lately. We were so looking forward to having you in our family . . . looking forward to beautiful grandchildren . . . Auntie Ronnie asked after you the other day and I just didn't know what to say . . . she says you should keep the beer glasses she gave you for the engagement. I suppose it's just as well she decided against the doona cover, I mean you'd be flat out dividing that in half wouldn't you? Now cheer up . . . come on . . . you're welcome around here anytime . . . you know that, don't you? Honestly he wouldn't know . . . it's about time he grew up. He was over here last night with some new woman in tow . . . blonde, quite attractive, but hardly his type. He needs someone more like you . . . a homebody . . . not someone who swans around here in a mini skirt as if she owns the place and none of the neighbours can keep their eyes off her. She just won't fit in around here . . . an exotic dancer, honestly! He can't seem to see what he's gotten himself into . . . he just follows her around like some lovestruck puppy. Now you just stop that . . . we'll still be here . . . even if he's traipsing off to some island with this woman . . . why don't you come up the hills with Auntie Ronnie and me next weekend for the tulip festival . . . that will put the bloom back in your cheeks . . . oh, I think that might have been a joke . . . tulip . . . bloom. Did you hear that, Ronnie? I'm on the phone, to Robert's girlfriend . . . no . . . not the blonde one . . . the other one. No, I've told her she can keep the beer glasses. Are you still there pet . . . hello . . . hello . . .?

DO'S AND DONT'S FOR THE NEWLY SINGLE

• Do not, under any circumstances, sleep with your Ex. Of course, the first thing you want to do when you are feeling lonely and sad is to run to the source of your greatest joy and comfort. But now is not the time. Later when your Ex has become an old and valued friend rather than a rancid heartbreaker you can share life's disappointments with him or her in a kind and dispassionate way (don't hold your breath on this one!). But right now a sympathetic head on the shoulder, a caring hand on the knee, will inevitably lead to a desperate face in the crotch, further entanglement and more pain.

Leave your Ex out of your sexual reveries. Think about anyone . . . Prince Edward, if you're really hard up. Picture your Ex when he's lost all his hair, except for what's on his back. Imagine her fifteen kilos heavier and sounding like her mother.

You are an addict, kid. Your Ex is the drug. Try to go cold turkey on this if you can. But since this is the most useless piece of advice in this whole book and it's inevitable you will go back for one last fuck, DON'T DO IT AGAIN!

• Don't go away to an idyllic retreat by yourself to recover. Run to the bosom of family and friends, a new absorbing job, join the circus or the Sandinistas. Don't go to a tropical resort or a mountain retreat with a pile of books and a diary promising yourself you will recover with dignity. There's no dignity to be had in this whole situation. The books will not be read, the glorious sunsets will be ignored, your drinks bill will be enormous, your telephone bill the size of the Chilean national debt. Besides, at beaches and mountains there are too many things to jump off.

• Do throw yourself on the mercy of your friends. All that 'stiff upper lip' stuff leads to bowel obstructions, hair loss and cancer, so the experts say. Find a friend who cares, and really fall apart. A good friend will drop everything and come running with tissues, champagne, joke books and exotic drugs. One of the silver linings of personal disaster is finding that people do want to help share your load and feel needed. Besides it's a sort of insurance policy for when it's their turn to be a loser.

Good friends will listen endlessly when you go over and over the same boring details. They never agree when you say, 'I've been such a fool'. They tell you how lucky you are to be rid of that small pile of excrement you used to call your lover. (And they think it's 'absolutely marvellous' should you ever get back together.) They say you've never looked better when you have sleepless eyes and three-day-old mascara. They'll tell you to 'shut up for Christ's sake' when you really are being a self-indulgent prat.

And if you've run out of friends who can bear to hear you drone on again and again there's always therapy. The opening gambit, 'Well, my Jungian analyst says . . .' is always a good one at dinner parties. People always think you must be in a higher income bracket than they had first imagined.

• Don't go anywhere you know your Ex will be, unless accompanied by a lawyer. You can easily fool yourself here. Today just happens to be a nice day and you just happen to feel like driving the long way home from work. Even if it does take you past your Ex's bus stop, so what?

There is no satisfaction to be had from this sort of adolescent behaviour.

The options are:

a) Your Ex looks utterly depressed and you feel responsible.

b) Your Ex looks fantastically happy and you feel suicidal.

c) Your Ex is holding hands with someone new and you feel you must drive into the back of the car in front of you.

If you really do want to keep tabs on what your Ex is up to there are a number of reputable private detective agencies for this sort of thing. But a word of warning: be prepared for what they may find out. That your place in the bed has been taken by an entire visiting Chinese basketball team may be something you didn't need to know. On the other hand, it may be just the information you were waiting on before alerting the media.

• Do take this opportunity to vent your anger on any of your Ex's personal possessions that were left behind. There are few sounds more soothing to the savage breast than those of photos ripping, sleeves being rent from shirts and heels being twisted off shoes. Records melt down into interesting shapes and books make good bonfires—ask any unhinged religious zealot. That quaint little piece of china your Ex picked up at an antique auction and you have always despised will suddenly seem worth the ridiculous amount of money it cost when it is pushed off a balcony. If you really must keep some mementoes, try placing them on an altar in the middle of a pentangle and riding around on a goat at midnight shouting, 'Die, Oh Evil One'. This will be far more entertaining than turning to the church in your hour of need.

PS: If you quite liked your Ex you might like to ring a removal company which offers reasonable rates.

PHONE CALL NO. 136
THE EX'S BEST FRIEND

Hello? Oh, it's you. What do you want? I don't know, you'll have to talk to her yourself. Look, what can I say? She's having a really hard time at the moment and I really think you have done enough damage, don't

you? She's gone away for a few weeks. We all decided she really needed a break and we made sure she got on that plane. I'm not allowed to tell you. If she wanted you to know she would have told you herself! It's just lucky that she's had me around. God knows what she would have done to herself if I hadn't been there to get her through. And I can tell you, I've made damn sure she hasn't called you. Every time she tried to pick up that phone I talked her out of it. There's nothing to be gained by you two thrashing this out. Jane is one of the most sensitive, intelligent and talented people I know. You two just aren't compatible. At last she's back with people who are more her type and who really do care about her. All right, if you really do want to send her a letter post it to me. Make sure you put enough stamps on and mark it, 'Care Of Falklands Island Post Office . . .'

'I got some Araldite . . . you know, that incredibly strong glue . . . and I glued stuff all over his car—bottle tops, chicken shit, sticks, cigarette butts—anything I could find in the front yard. I did it in the middle of the night. I would have liked to see his face when he found it in the morning.'

JANICE, 27. SHOP ASSISTANT.

The odds are six to five that the light at the end of the tunnel is an oncoming train. PAUL DICKSON

Well, what's left to say? You've cut your hair, spent your money, ruined your health, moved away, built bonfires, run up a huge phone bill, wreaked all kinds of emotional havoc on everyone you know, cried, kicked and then cried some more. And you still feel bad. The only thing left is time.

The brokenhearted have a torrid affair with time. It doesn't run in its usual tidy way according to the calendar. Time becomes a deceptive master, full of treacherous tricks. Last year is as close as yesterday. Last week is lost in the mist. Tomorrow is a lifetime away. Today is taking forever and what time is it now?

Yes, time will conspire to really fuck you over. You'll be starting to feel better and the tulips will come up, those tulips you and Gary planted in the winter right where you could see them from your bedroom window. You tell everyone you're over it and that song will blast out on the radio and all you can see is Helen eating spaghetti and laughing at your jokes.

'Time heals all', your mother will say. Remember this is from the same woman who said, 'Eat your carrots and you'll see in the dark'. It's also from the woman who looks dreamily into the distance when she talks about the lover who, thirty years ago, broke her heart before she met your father, the man who ruined her life.

Time doesn't heal you completely after a car crash—you're left with a limp or a steel plate in your head. And time won't heal you after a multiple passion pile-up on the highway of life. It's been said that grief is more like a physical injury than any other type of illness. The lovelorn talk about being 'torn apart', 'wounded', 'hit hard'. And maybe you shouldn't expect a full recovery anyway. You'll be left with something . . . two kids, tyre marks across your torso, a tattoo on your chest reading *Sue Forever*, a limp or a steel plate in your head. That old you who was in love with whatsaname is gone and a new you exists. Maybe it's a you who needs to get hit once more before you know not to play in the traffic. Maybe it's a you who enjoys hit and run accidents. But hopefully it's a new, wiser you who knows to get off the highway when you see a heavy articulated love truck bearing down.

PS: You'll probably be looking for a new relationship round about now, but as we all know there is a period of ritual humiliation to be endured first. Now is the time to start dating and sleeping with all the no-hopers, weirdos and wimps you wouldn't ordinarily touch with a barge pole. This humiliation thing is one of life's lovely touches. It's so that when you do finally meet someone you really like you appreciate it much more.

Here's a handy guide to the sort of folk you never knew existed, but whom you will be spending most of your time with in the near future:

The brokenhearted.

You will find that you have an irresistible attraction for people who are as screwed up as you are. You will agree to meet for dinner with unreasonable haste and with expectations of a miraculous love cure running high. Even before entrée is cleared away you will both be revealing the intimate details of your past disaster and comparing notes. Just leave early and cut your losses. Sex is not possible without one or both of you bursting into tears. Besides, 'Oh God, yes, Brian' is not what you want to hear when your name is Trevor.

People who like you more than you like them. People you like more than they like you.

This category makes up almost ninety per cent of the population and therefore can't be avoided, but should be taken in small doses.

Waiters, taxi drivers, bar persons, cloakroom attendants, bouncers.

This is a group you will have increasing contact with as you lurch from one sleazy nightspot to another in search of who knows what. Remember their night is made up of people like you, they never look quite as cute under proper lighting and you will have passed out by the time they get off work anyway. They also expect tips.

Marrieds.

People who are married can spot a bereaved soul who needs comforting a mile off. They calculate they can get you into bed and home in a taxi before you've really had time to think it through, and they're right. If one of these vultures preys on you, the least you can do is a *Fatal Attraction* number on their kid's pet. Don't feel guilty about this, it's probably just what they need to put the zing back into their relationship.

The chronically single.

When people introduce themselves with the information that they've been celibate for years and years, there's bound to be a good reason. Let some other sucker find out. You may imagine that sex with a celibate will be extraordinary . . . think of all that pent-up passion! It's more likely they've actually forgotten how to do it. Exit discreetly and let them have sex with someone they really love . . . themselves.

Cheap and nasty substitutes can be fun for a while, but try to hang out till something worthwhile comes along. Don't forget you are now the envy of half the population—those who are in a relationship. Watch the couples at the dinner table look longingly at you when you announce that you might kick on at a nightclub and dance with strangers. This single life could be fun.

And more importantly, you now have the chance to experience the heady delights of falling in love all over again.

This is a Love Gone Wrong song
How did your love go wrong?
Did he leave you for the woman next door?
How did your love go wrong?

Did she fall in love with your best friend?
Did you lose your legs in the war?
Was it an unfortunate end to a dirty weekend?
Was it your mother-in-law?

This is a Love Gone Wrong song.
How did your love go wrong?
Did you have a change of heart, just drift apart?
How did your love go wrong?

Was it just that you weren't ready?
Was it physical and didn't last?
Was it merely that passion seemed out of fashion?
A dark secret out of your past?

This is a Love Gone Wrong song.
How did your love go wrong?
Were you just weak and stupid, tripped up the Cupid?
How did your love go wrong?

Thanks to:

PHILLIP, PAUL
PATRICK, JEN
LOUIS, DALE
HUGH, HILARY, KATE